TRAVIS
GOOD FEELING

GUITAR
T A B
EDITION

SONY MUSIC PUBLISHING

GW00455236

Exclusive Distributors:
Music Sales Limited
8/9 Frith Street, London W1D 3JB, England.
Music Sales Pty Limited
120 Rothschild Avenue, Rosebery, NSW 2018, Australia.

Order No. AM964469
ISBN 0-7119-8289-9
This book © Copyright 2001 by Sony Music Publishing.

Music arranged by Richard Barrett.
Music engraved by Digital Music Art.
Printed in the United Kingdom by
Caligraving Limited, Thetford, Norfolk.

Your Guarantee of Quality:
As publishers, we strive to produce every
book to the highest commercial standards.
The music has been freshly engraved and,
whilst endeavouring to retain the original running
order of the recorded album, the book has been
carefully designed to minimise awkward page
turns and to make playing from it a real pleasure.
Particular care has been given to specifying
acid-free, neutral-sized paper made from pulps
which have not been elemental chlorine bleached.
This pulp is from farmed substainable forests and
was produced with special regard for the environment.
Throughout, the printing and binding have been
planned to ensure a sturdy, attractive publication
which should give years of enjoyment.
If your copy fails to meet our high standards,
please inform us and we will gladly replace it.

Music Sales' complete catalogue describes
thousands of titles and is available in full colour
sections by subject, direct from Music Sales Limited.
Please state your areas of interest and send
a cheque/postal order for £1.50 for postage to:
Music Sales Limited, Newmarket Road,
Bury St. Edmunds, Suffolk IP33 3YB.

www.musicsales.com

Guitar Tablature Explained

Guitar music can be notated three different ways: on a musical stave, in tablature, and in rhythm slashes

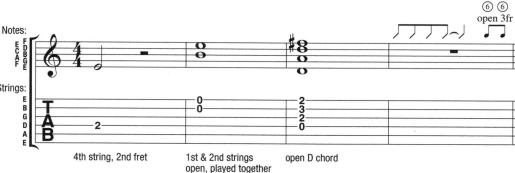

RHYTHM SLASHES are written above the stave. Strum chords in the rhythm indicated. Round noteheads indicate single notes.

THE MUSICAL STAVE shows pitches and rhythms and is divided by lines into bars. Pitches are named after the first seven letters of the alphabet.

TABLATURE graphically represents the guitar fingerboard. Each horizontal line represents a string, and each number represents a fret.

4th string, 2nd fret   1st & 2nd strings open, played together   open D chord

Definitions for special guitar notation

SEMI-TONE BEND: Strike the note and bend up a semi-tone (1/2 step).

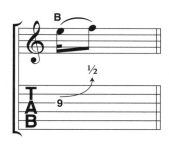

WHOLE-TONE BEND: Strike the note and bend up a whole-tone (whole step).

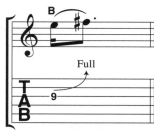

GRACE NOTE BEND: Strike the note and bend as indicated. Play the first note as quickly as possible.

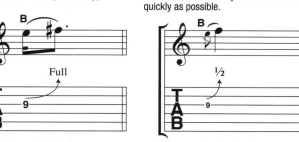

QUARTER-TONE BEND: Strike the note and bend up a 1/4 step.

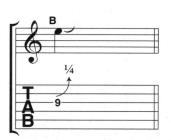

BEND & RELEASE: Strike the note and bend up as indicated, then release back to the original note.

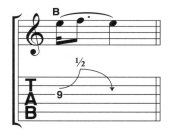

BEND & RESTRIKE: Strike the note and bend as indicated then restrike the string where the symbol occurs.

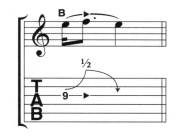

PRE-BEND: Bend the note as indicated, then strike it.

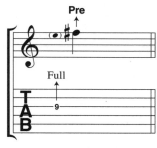

PRE-BEND & RELEASE: Bend the note as indicated. Strike it and release the note back to the original pitch.

HAMMER-ON: Strike the first (lower) note with one finger, then sound the higher note (on the same string) with another finger by fretting it without picking.

PULL-OFF: Place both fingers on the notes to be sounded. Strike the first note and without picking, pull the finger off to sound the second (lower) note.

LEGATO SLIDE (GLISS): Strike the first note and then slide the same fret-hand finger up or down to the second note. The second note is not struck.

SHIFT SLIDE (GLISS & RESTRIKE): Same as legato slide, except the second note is struck.

NATURAL HARMONIC: Strike the note while the fret-hand lightly touches the string directly over the fret indicated.

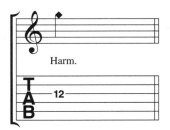

PICK SCRAPE: The edge of the pick is rubbed down (or up) the string, producing a scratchy sound.

PALM MUTING: The note is partially muted by the pick hand lightly touching the string(s) just before the bridge.

MUFFLED STRINGS: A percussive sound is produced by laying the fret hand across the string(s) without depressing, and striking them with the pick hand.

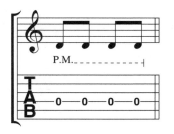

NOTE: The speed of any bend is indicated by the music notation and tempo.

All I Want To Do Is Rock

Words & Music by Fran Healy

5

I'll stay,— not walk— a - way.———

Verse

Hey,———— I'm a foot with-out a sock,- with-out—

Gtrs. 1+2+3

f Gtr. 1 w/dist.

— you.—

Love,————————— you seem to work a -

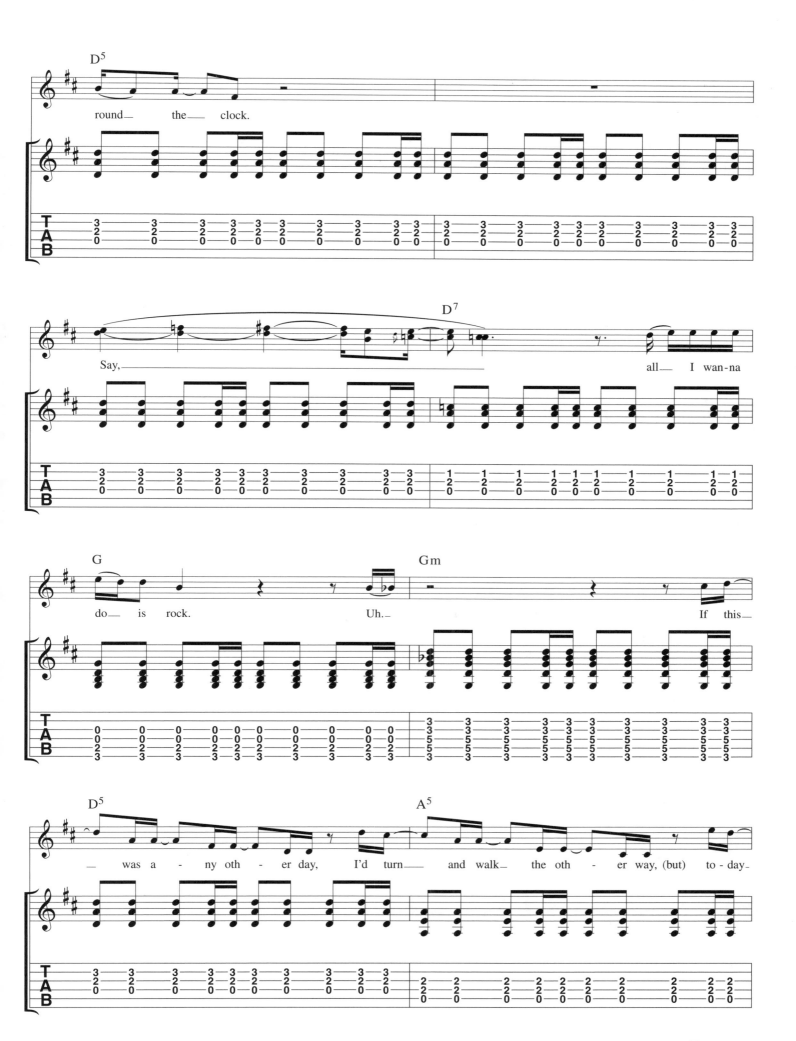

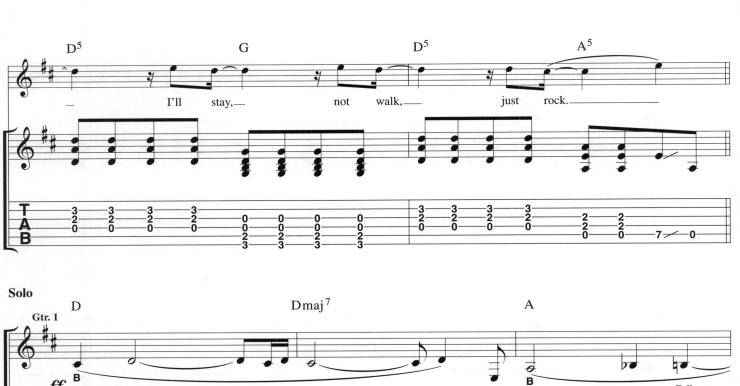

I'll stay,— not walk,— just rock._____

Solo

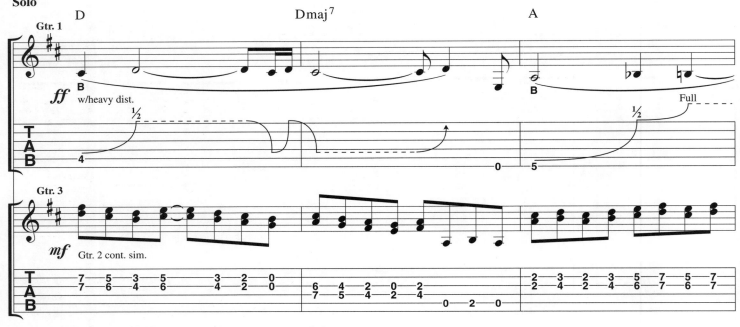

† (w/feedback)

† feedback indicated by cue notes in parentheses

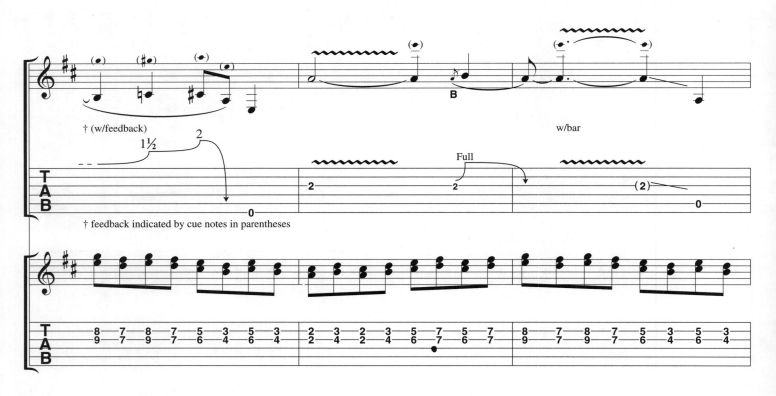

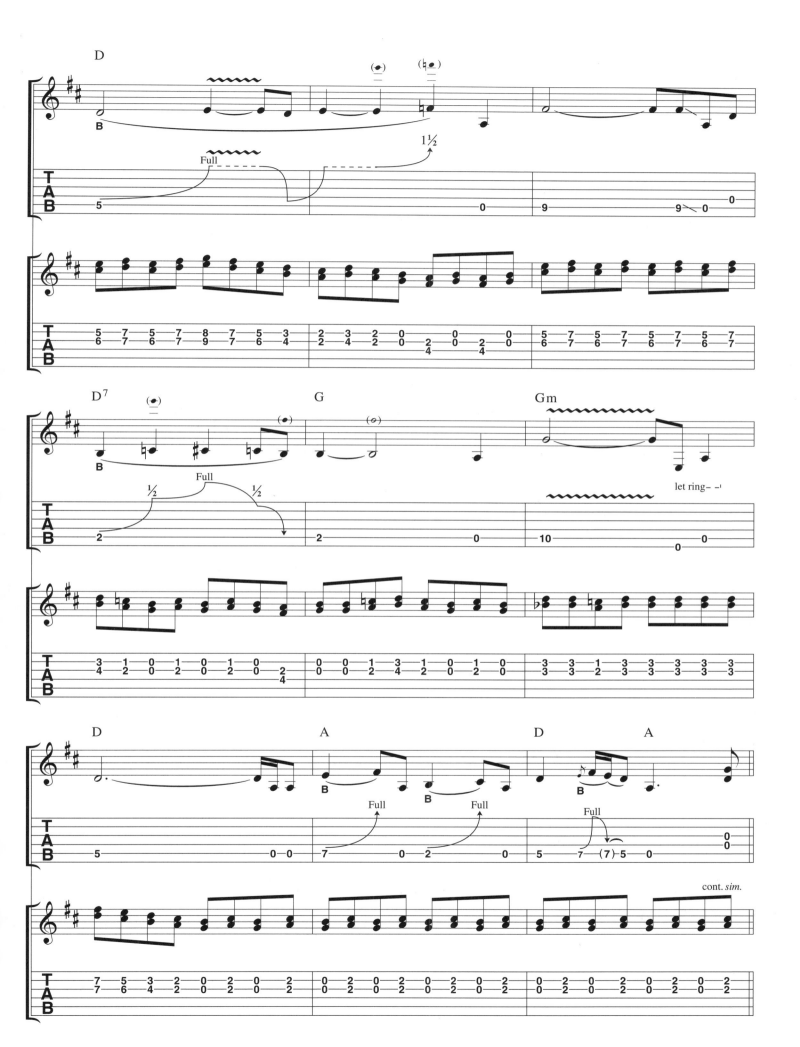

9

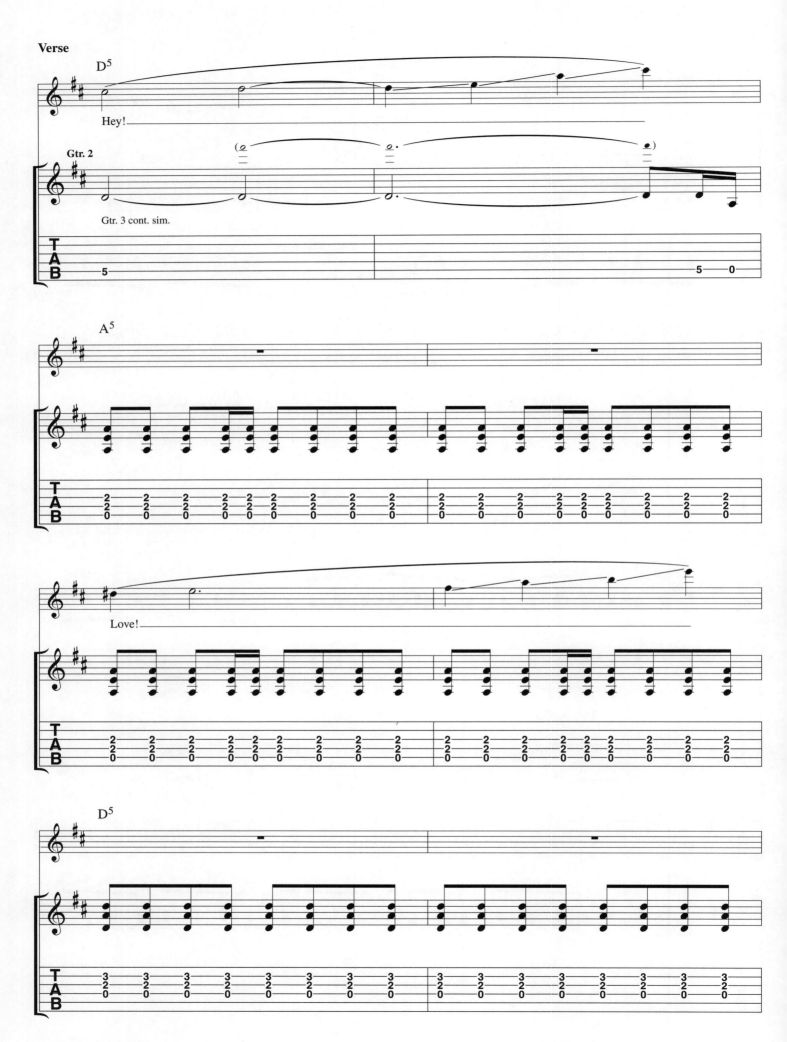

U16 Girls

Words & Music by Fran Healy

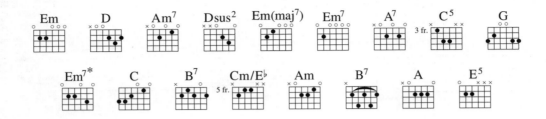

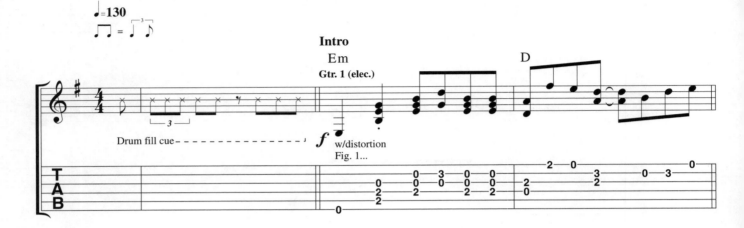

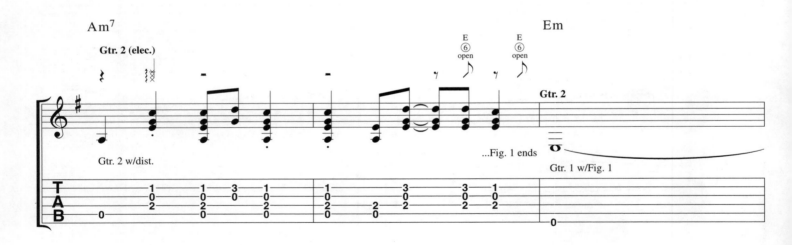

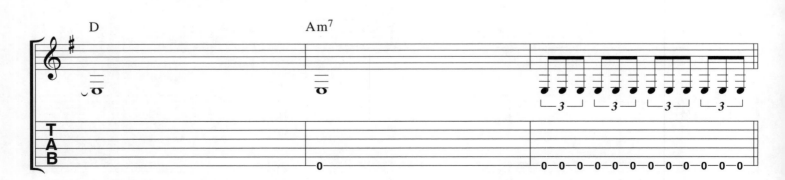

13

She was all ____ for all or no - thing, ____ (She was) o -
And her eyes ____ were full of dew drops, ____ the

- pen all ____ the time. ____ (But)
mo - ment I walked in. ____ She was

Bridge

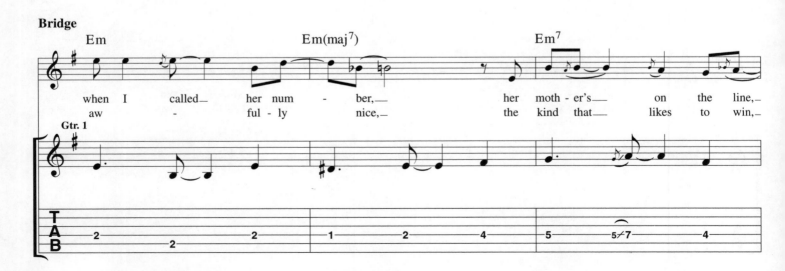

when I called ____ her num - ber, ____ her moth - er's ____ on the line,
aw - ful - ly nice, ____ the kind that ____ likes to win, ____

Gtr. 1

15

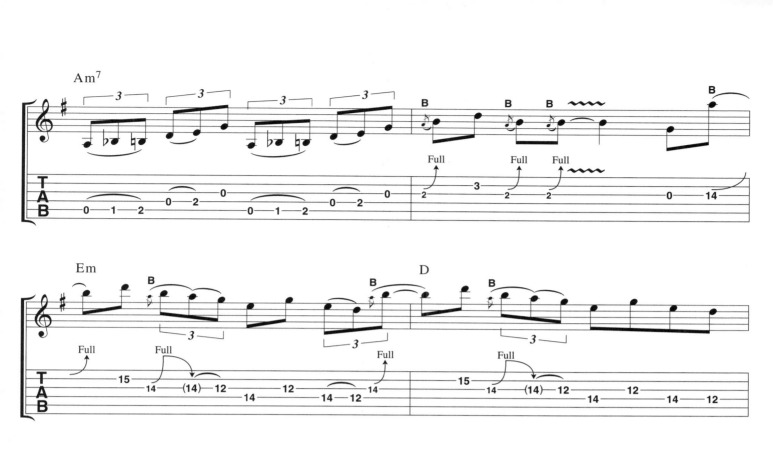

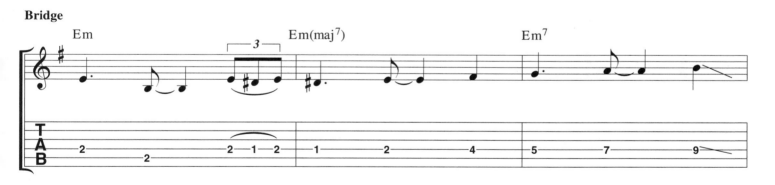

Bridge

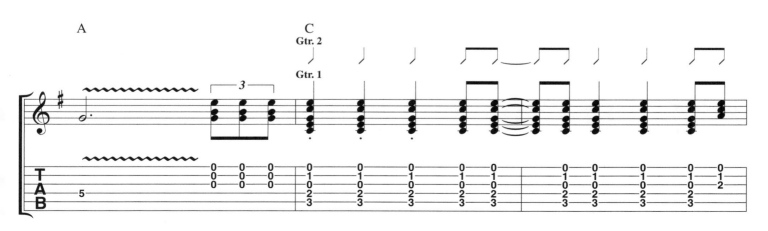

18

Good Day To Die

Words & Music by Fran Healy

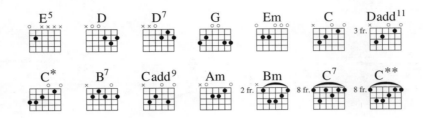

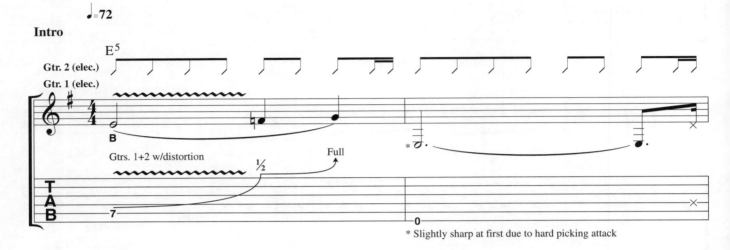

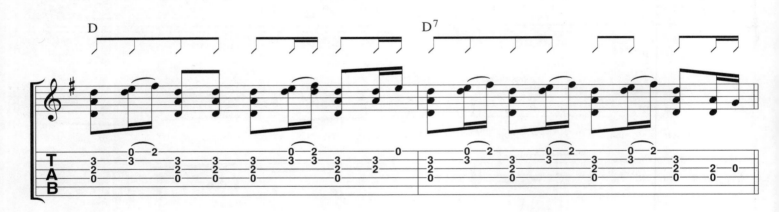

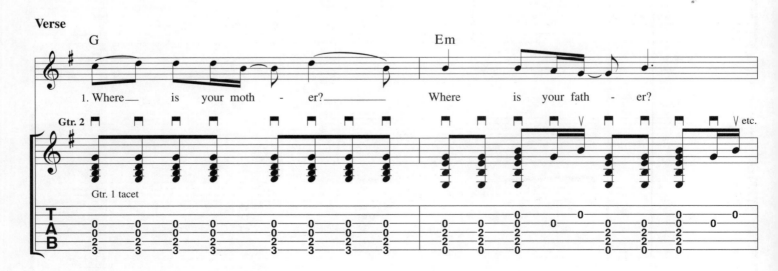

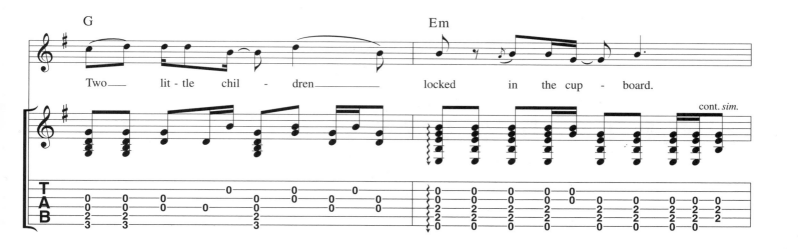

Two—   lit - tle   chil - dren——————   locked   in   the   cup - board.

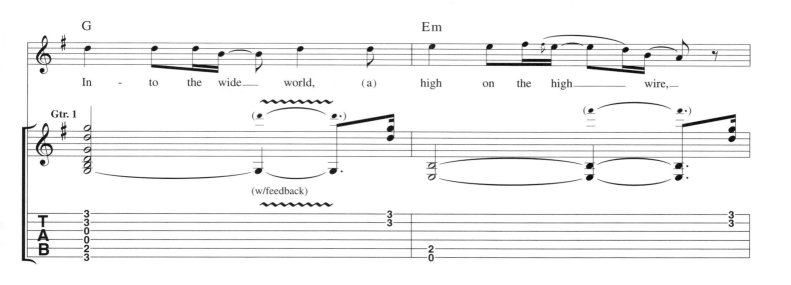

In - to   the   wide— world,   (a) high   on   the   high————— wire,—

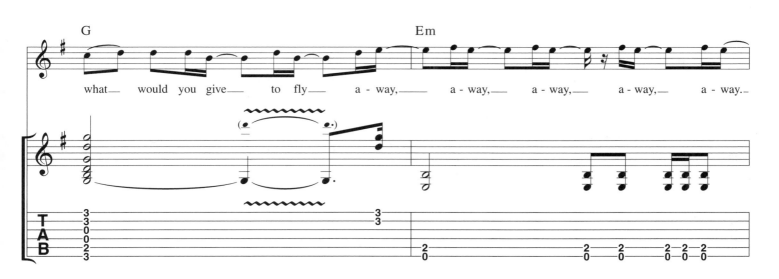

what— would you give— to fly— a - way,—   a - way,—   a - way,—   a - way,—   a - way.—

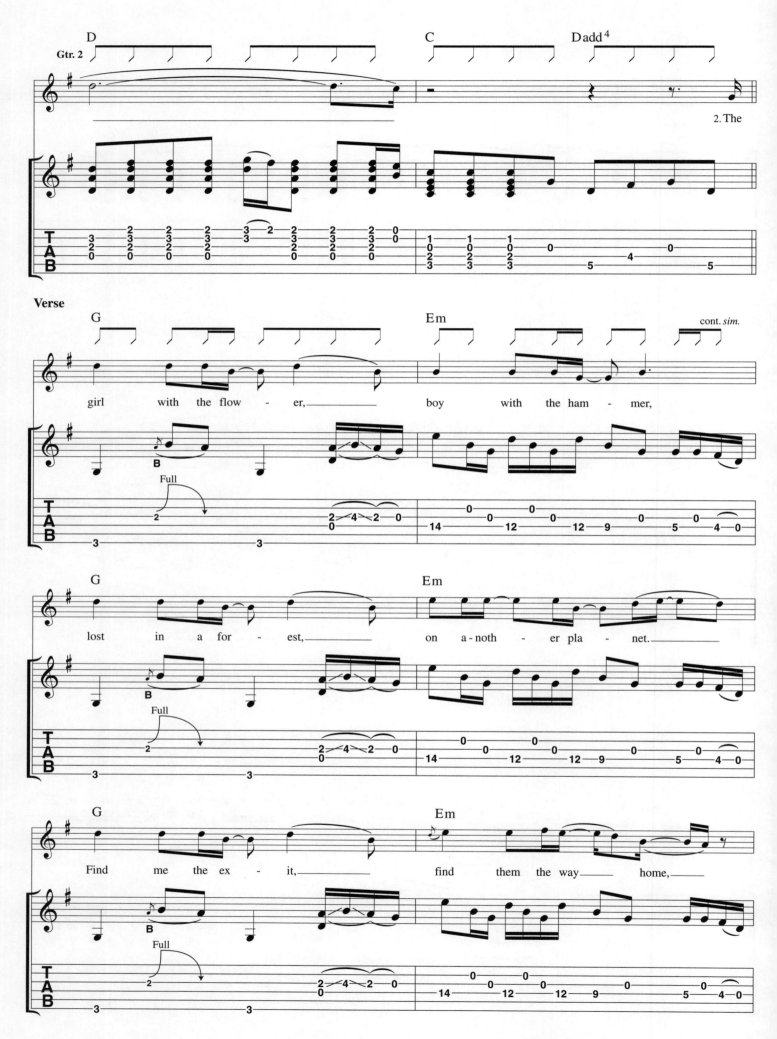

22

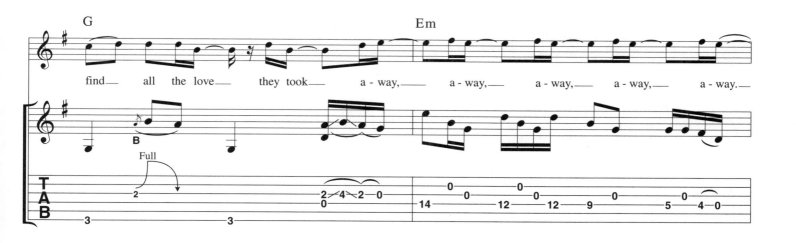

find— all the love— they took— a - way, a - way, a - way, a - way, a - way.—

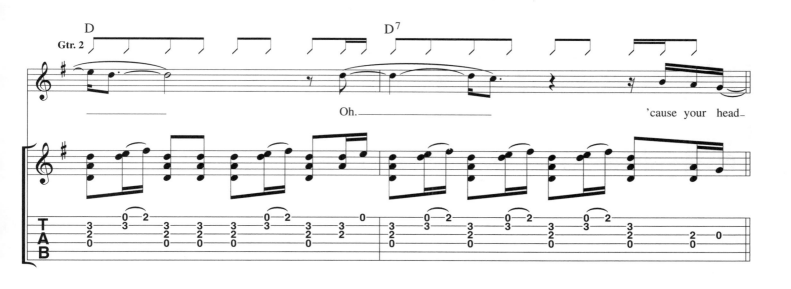

——————————— Oh.——————————— 'cause your head—

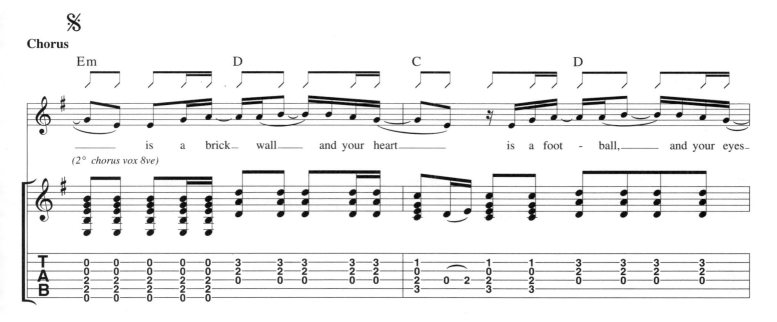

—— is a brick— wall— and your heart— is a foot - ball,— and your eyes—

(2° chorus vox 8ve)

Chorus

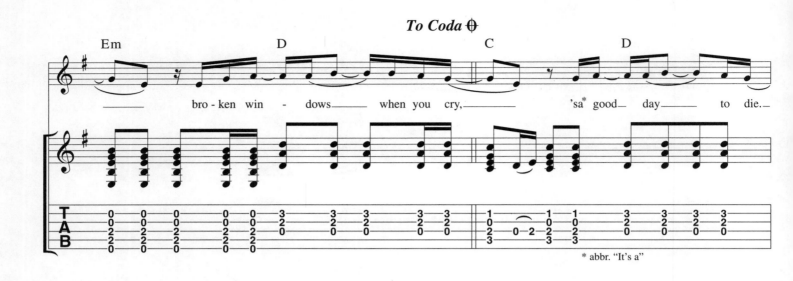

To Coda ⊕

* abbr. "It's a"

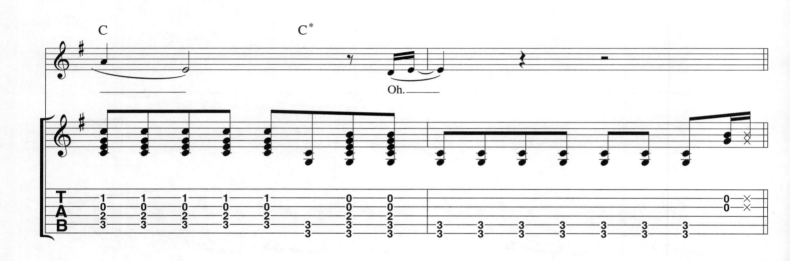

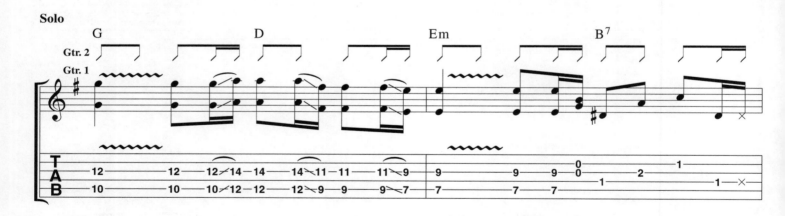

Solo

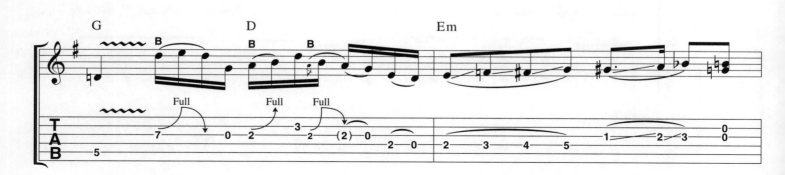

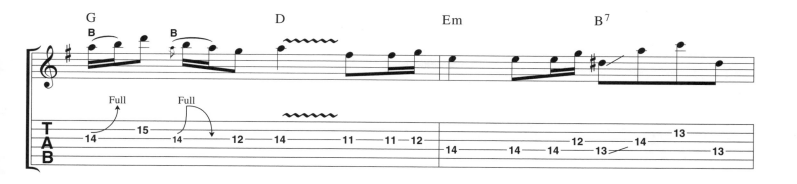

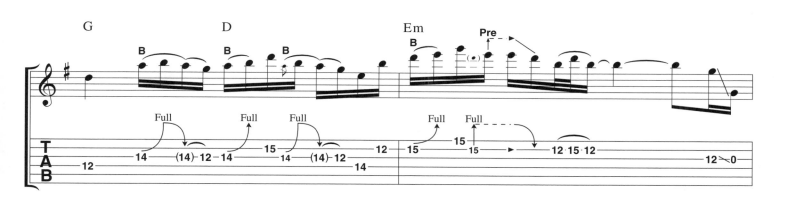

D.%. al Coda

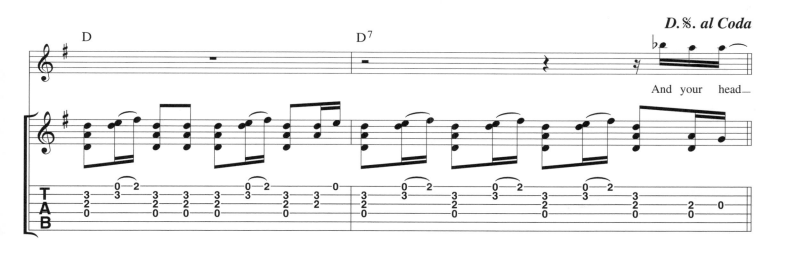

And your head—

Coda

——— 'sa good— day,—'cause your head— is a brick— wall— and your heart—

to die,—————————— to die.—

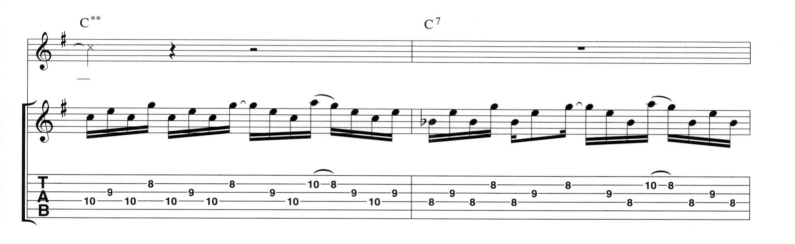

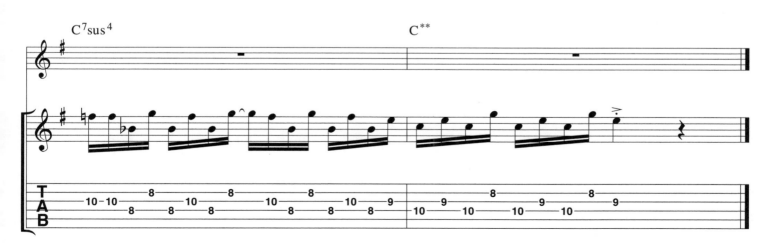

Good Feeling

Words & Music by Fran Healy

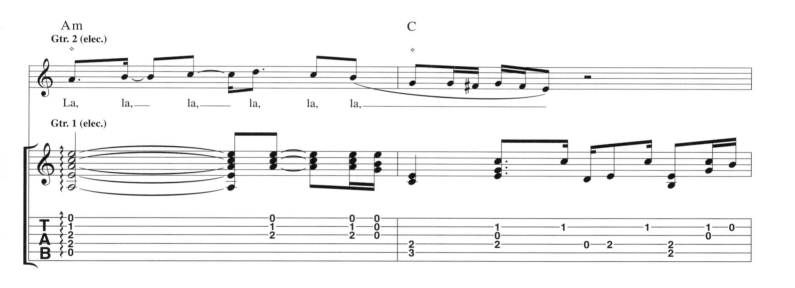

29

Verse

feel-ing____ like__ I know how I'm feel - ing,   scrap - ing me off the ceil - ing,   back__ to that

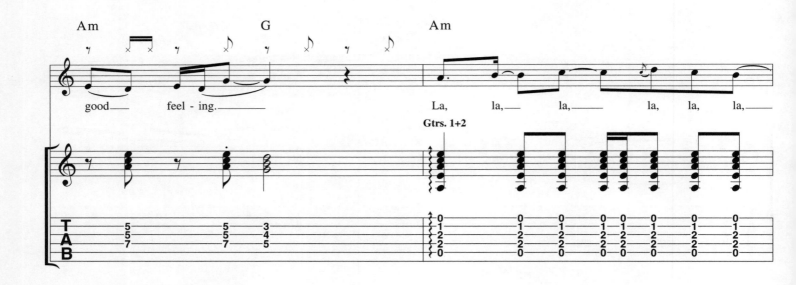

good____ feel - ing.____   La,   la,____ la,____   la, la, la,

Gtrs. 1+2

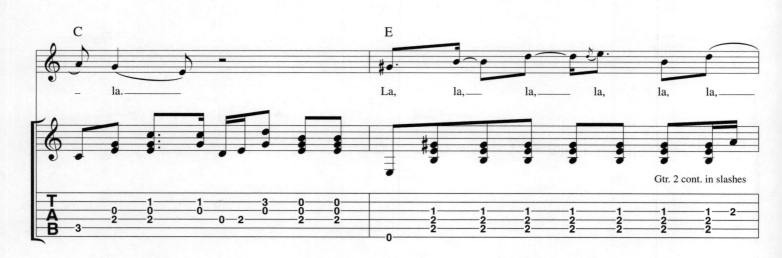

__ la.____   La,   la,____ la,____ la,   la, la,

Gtr. 2 cont. in slashes

la. ———

La, la, — la, —— la, la, la, —

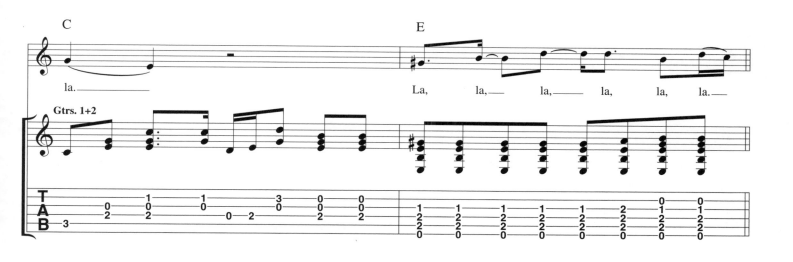

la. ———

La, la, — la, —— la, la, la. —

Middle 8

You picked a time, a ve-ry fine time, —— to look at me, you'd see that I was fine. —

Piano Solo

Piano arr. for Gtr.
(Gtr. 1 accents crotchet beats 2 + 4)

Outro

Now, I got a good_____ feel - in', like__ I know how I'm feel-ing, scrap - ing me

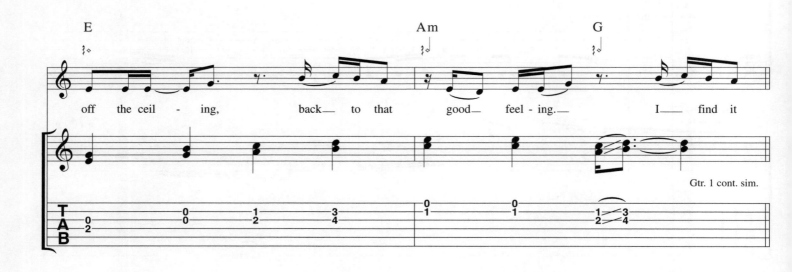

off the ceil - ing, back__ to that good__ feel - ing.__ I__ find it

hard__ liv-ing, wast - ing our time__ giv-ing, when__ will they all__

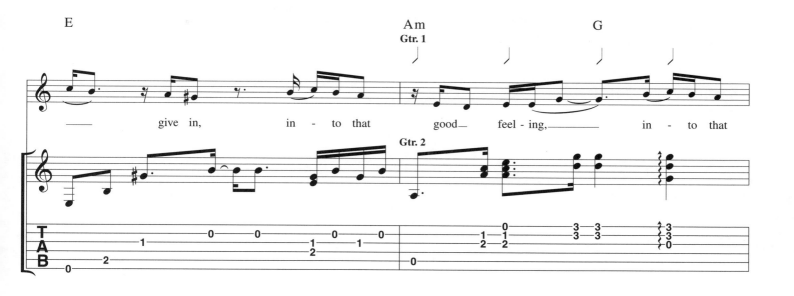

give in, in - to that good_ feel - ing,_____ in - to that

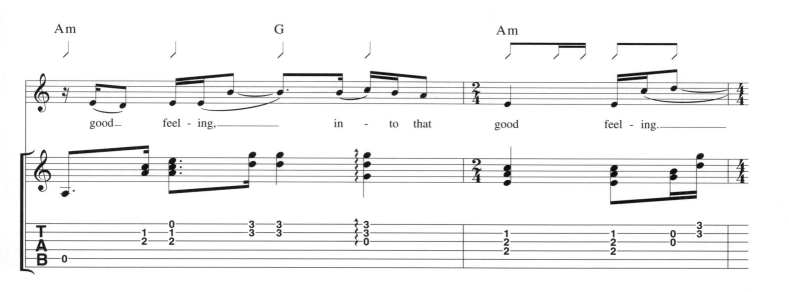

good_ feel - ing,_____ in - to that good feel - ing._____

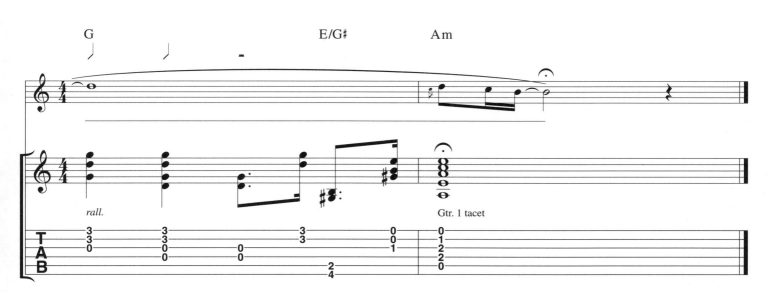

Midsummer Nights Dreamin'

Words & Music by Fran Healy

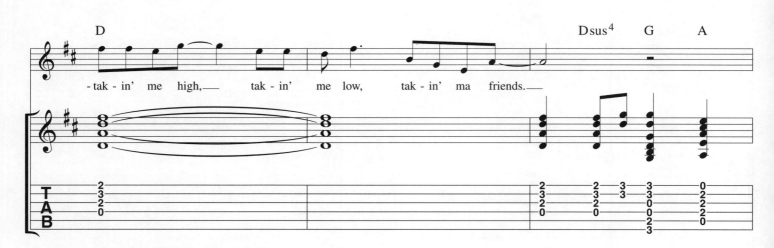

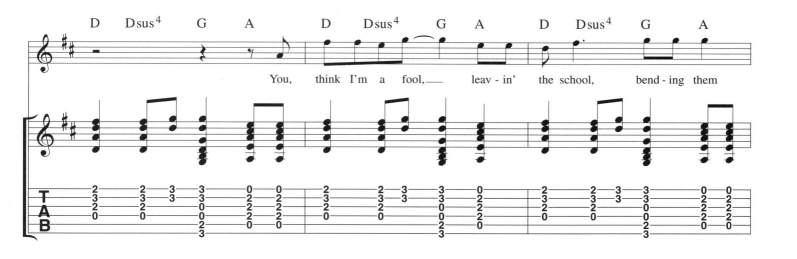

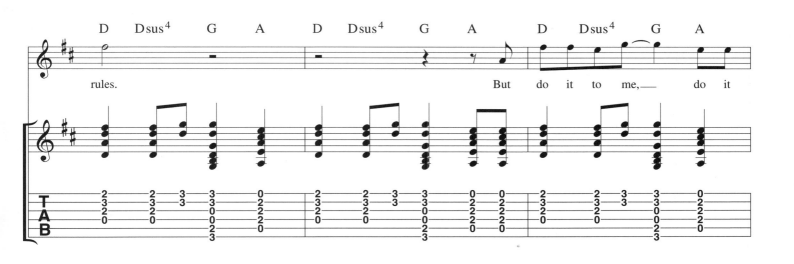

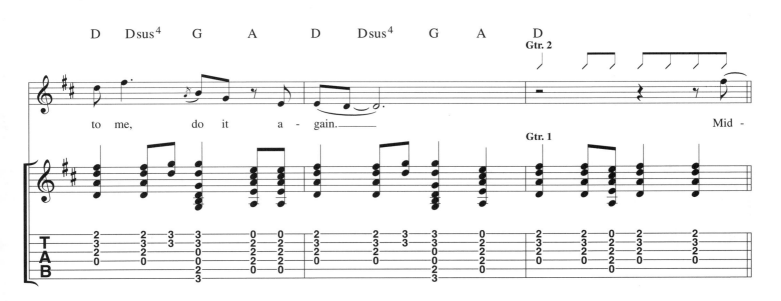

38

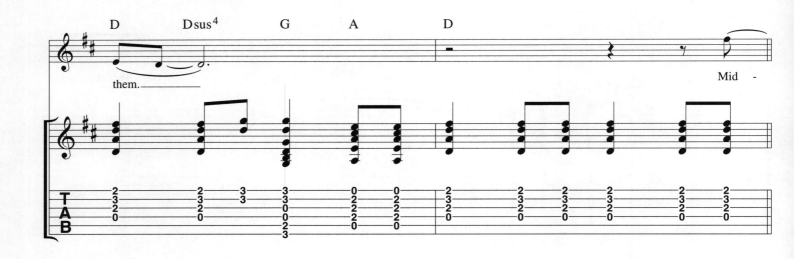

Chorus

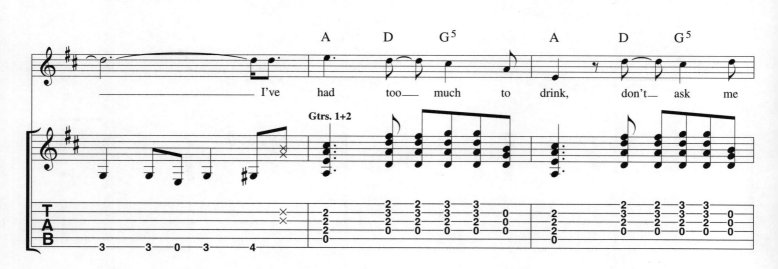

now,   head—   in   the——   sink.   Yeah!—

Solo

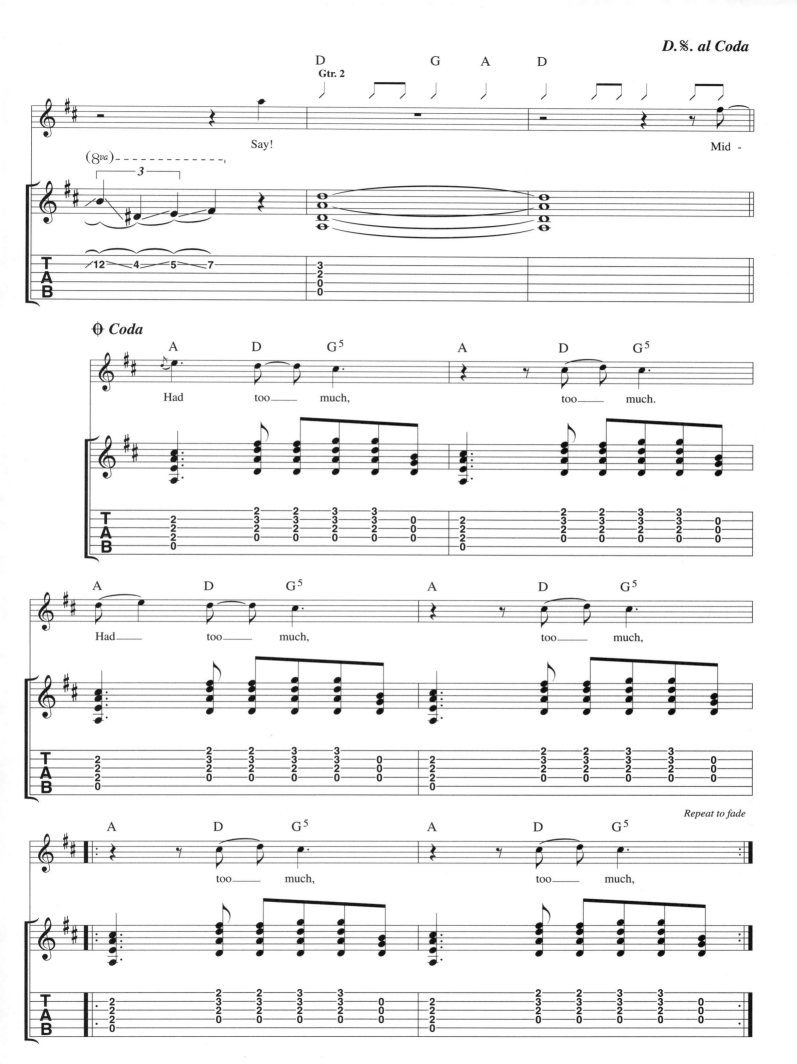

Tied To The 90's

Words & Music by Fran Healy

Verse

45

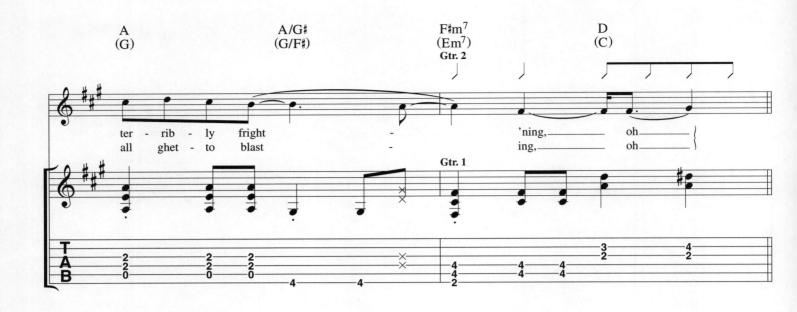

ter - rib - ly fright - 'ning,_____ oh _____
all ghet - to blast - ing,_____ oh _____

Bridge

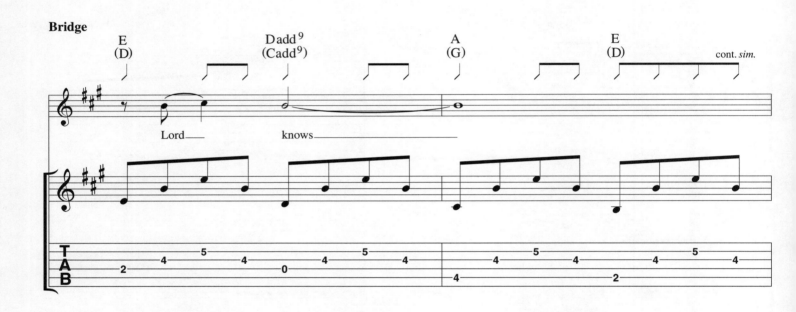

Lord_____ knows_____

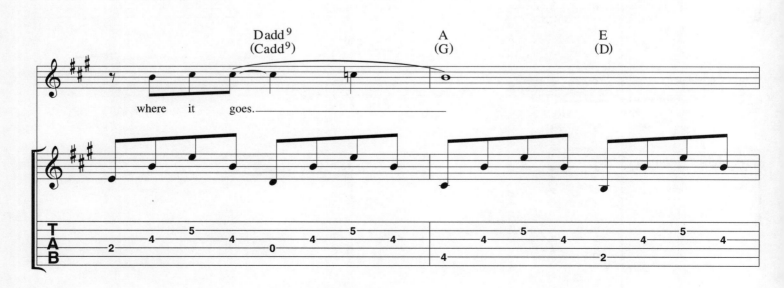

where it goes._____

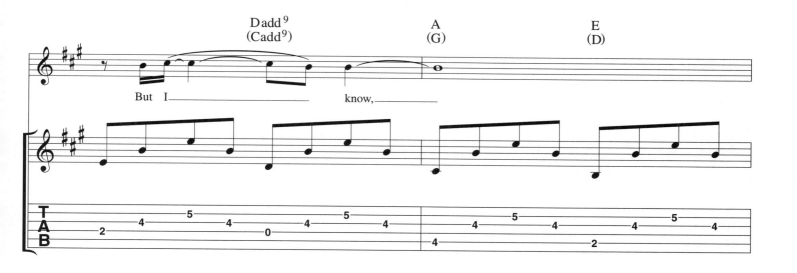

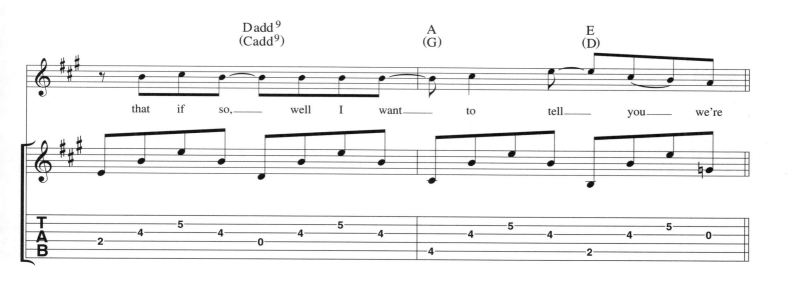

Chorus

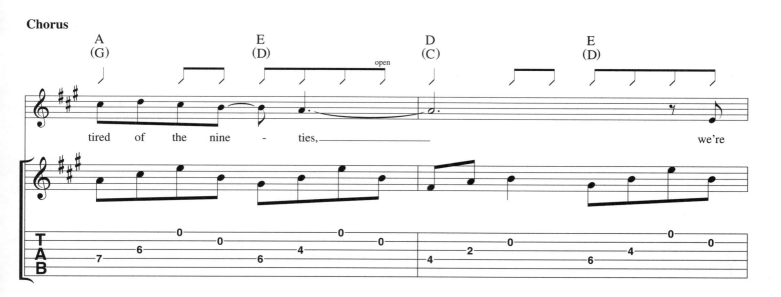

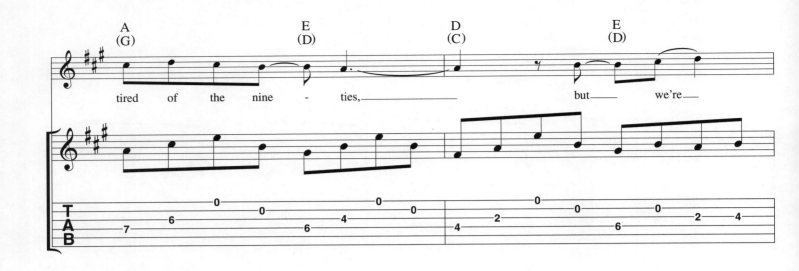

tired of the nine-ties, _____ _____ but _____ we're _____

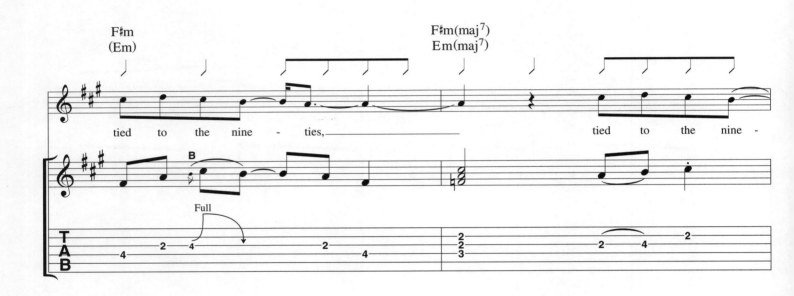

tied to the nine-ties, _____ _____ tied to the nine-

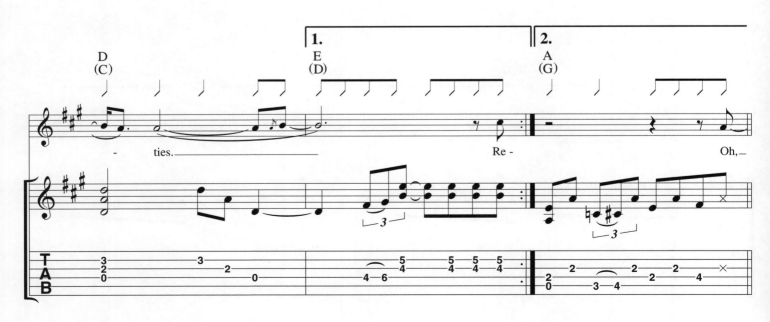

-ties. _____ _____ Re- Oh,—

48

Middle 8

oh, no, _____ it's not long to_____ go, on the

hi - fi five a - live._____

That's___ it,_____ I'm stay - in' in___ bed____ 'til my

hair falls out, ev - 'ry thing's___ old_____

50

51

Outro

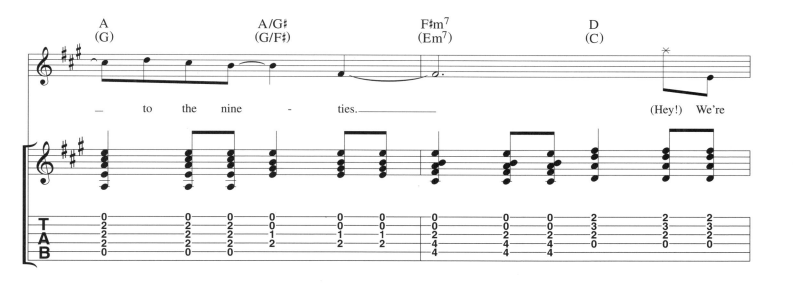

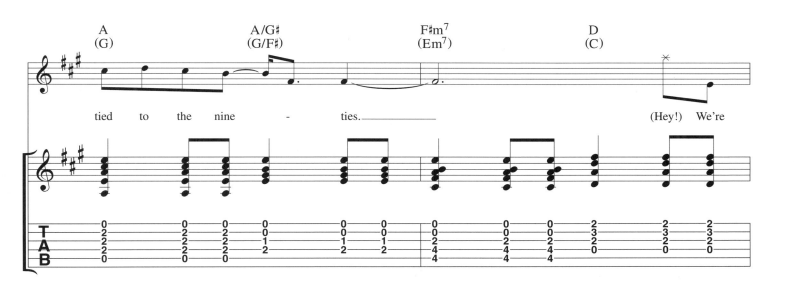

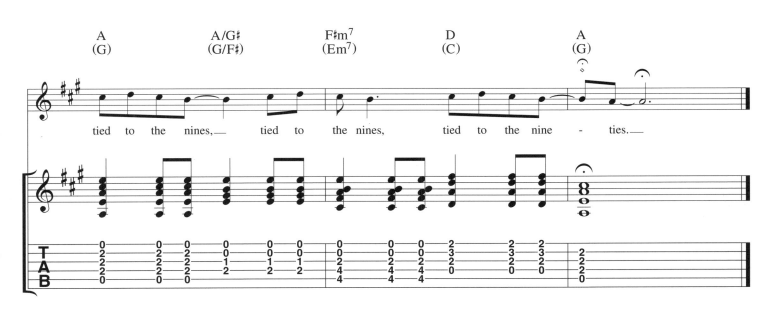

The Line Is Fine

Words & Music by Fran Healy

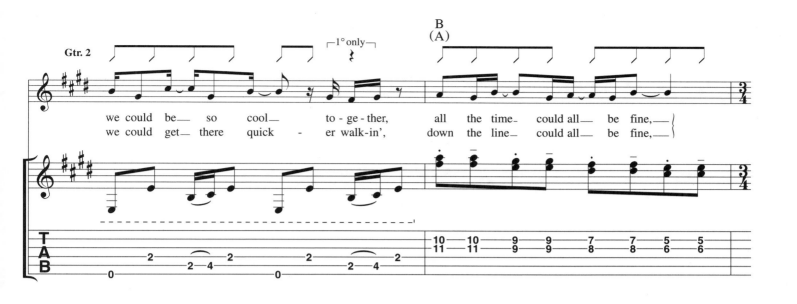

we could be__ so cool__ to - ge - ther, all the time__ could all__ be fine,__
we could get__ there quick - er walk-in', down the line__ could all__ be fine,__

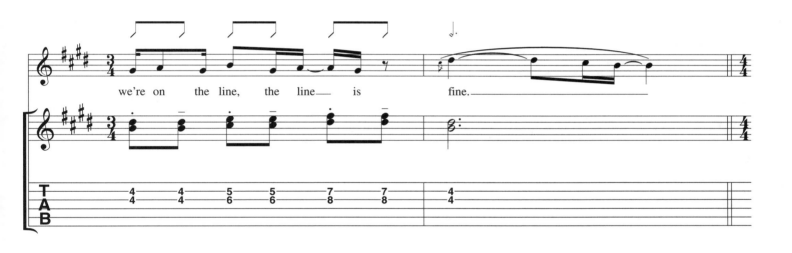

we're on the line, the line__ is fine.__

Chorus

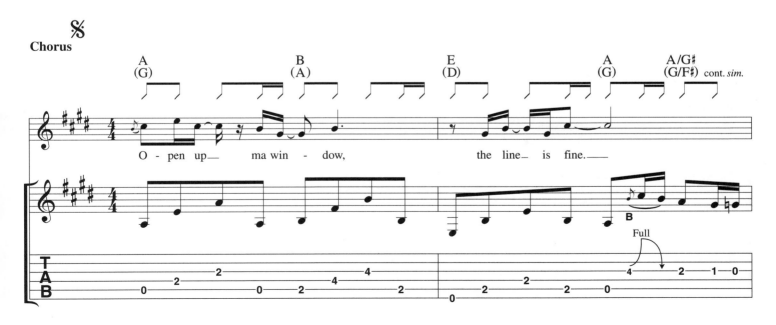

O - pen up__ ma win - dow, the line__ is fine.__

Stand - ing on the ledge, oh, well I don't look down.
(The line is fine.)

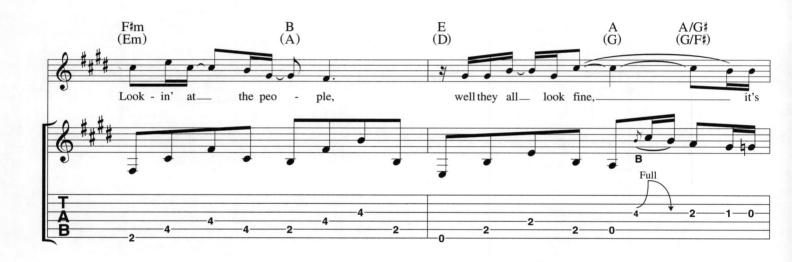

Look - in' at the peo - ple, well they all look fine, it's

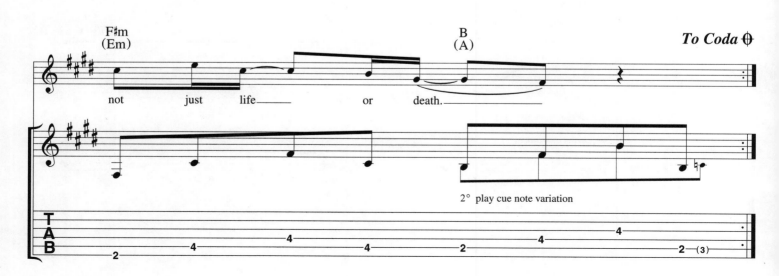

not just life or death.

To Coda ⊕

2° play cue note variation

56

Middle 8

Solo

but the line— is fine,_____ it's not just life— or death,_____

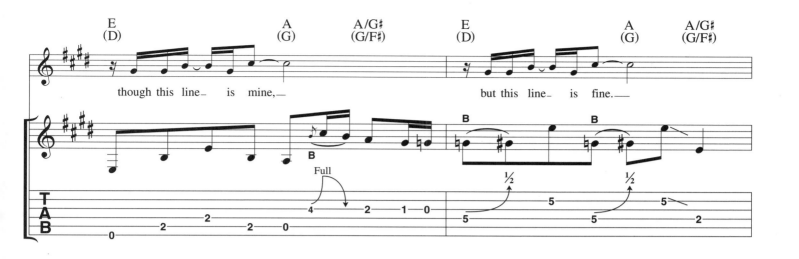

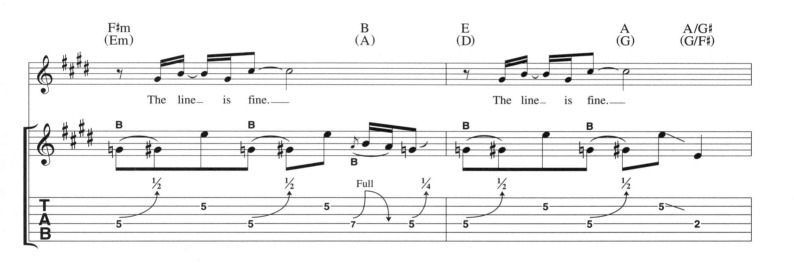

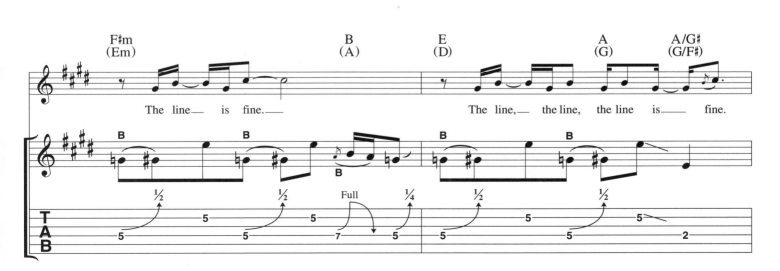

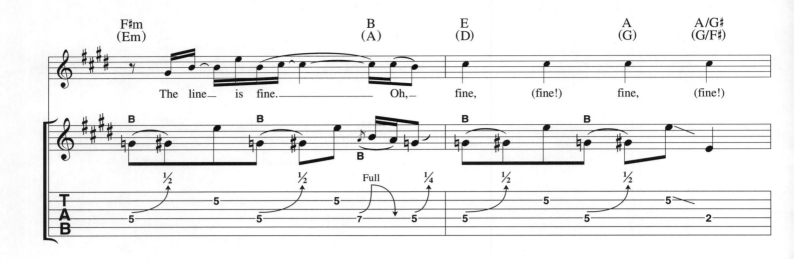

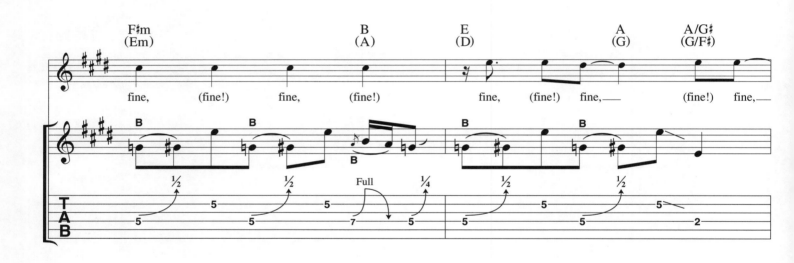

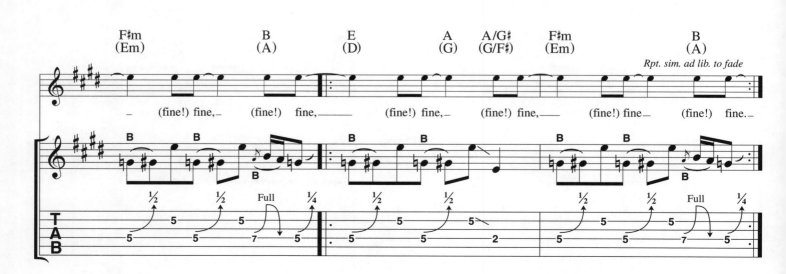

I Love You Anyways

Words & Music by Fran Healy

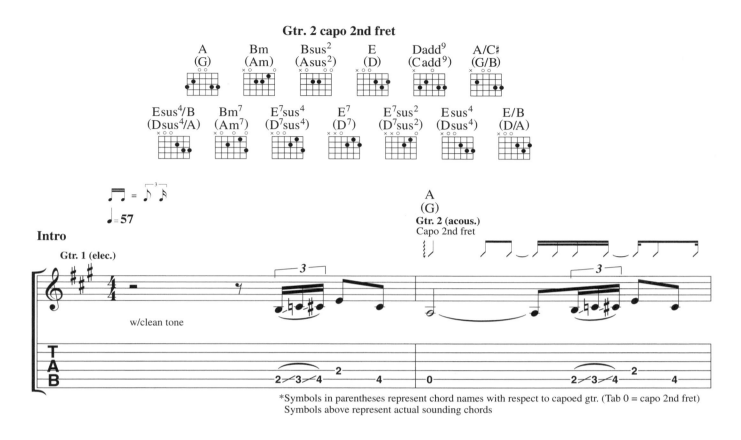

*Symbols in parentheses represent chord names with respect to capoed gtr. (Tab 0 = capo 2nd fret)
Symbols above represent actual sounding chords

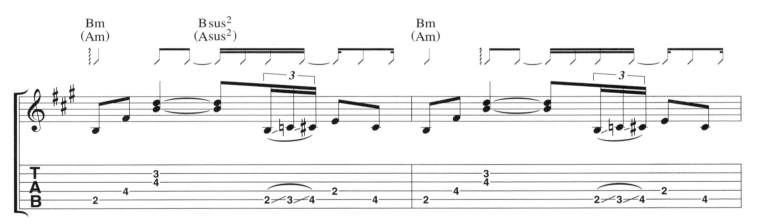

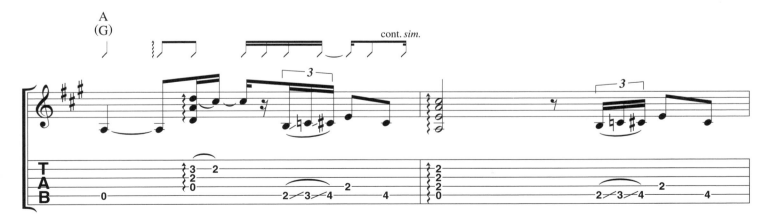

62

64

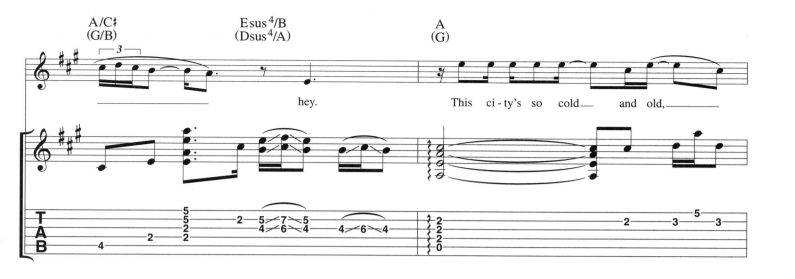

hey.   This ci-ty's so cold— and old,—

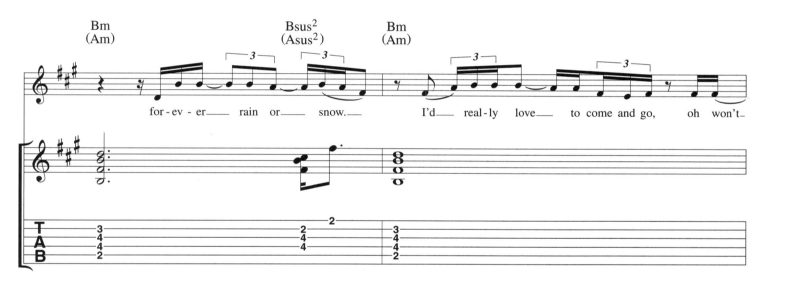

for-ev-er— rain or— snow.— I'd— real-ly love— to come and go,   oh won't—

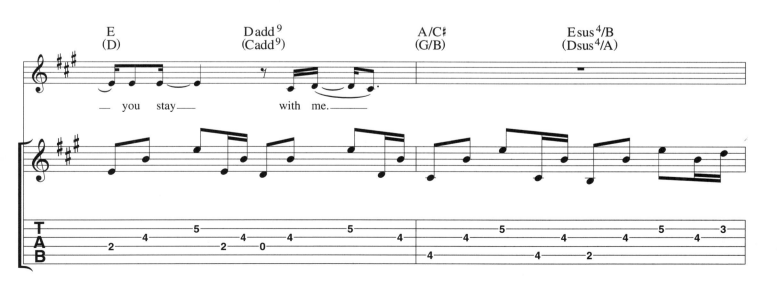

— you stay— with me.—

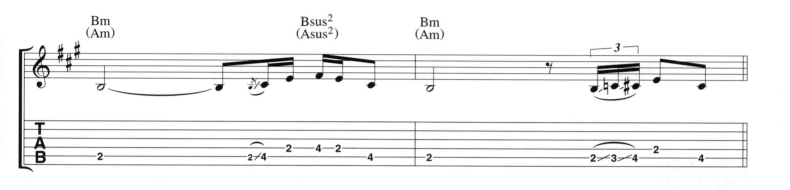

D.%. al Coda

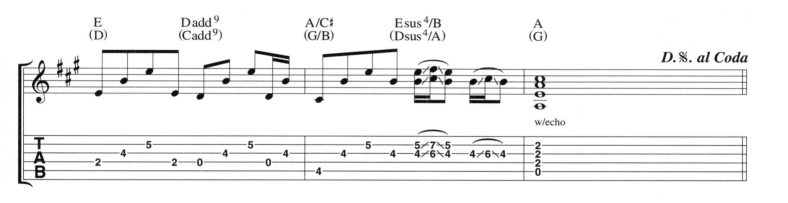

w/echo

𝄋 Coda

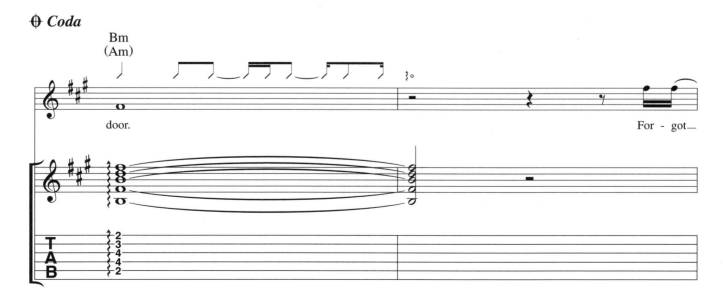

door.

For - got—

More Than Us

Words & Music by Fran Healy

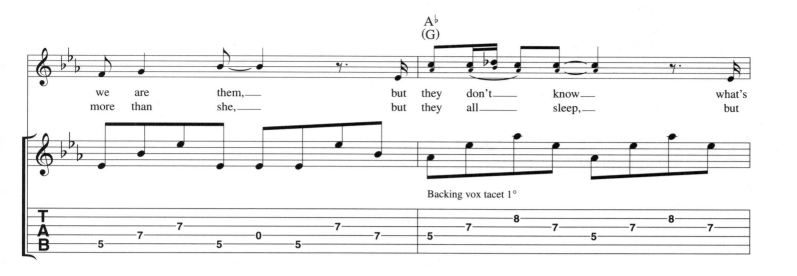

Backing vox tacet 1°

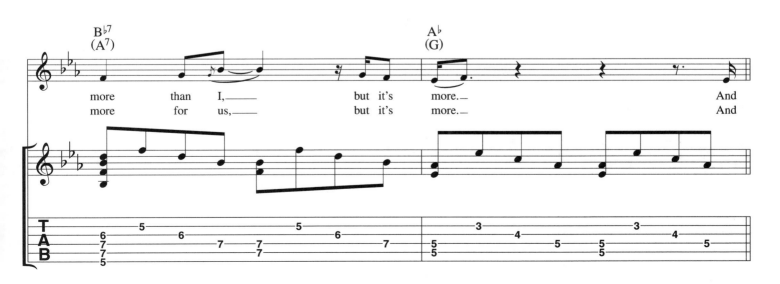

Bridge

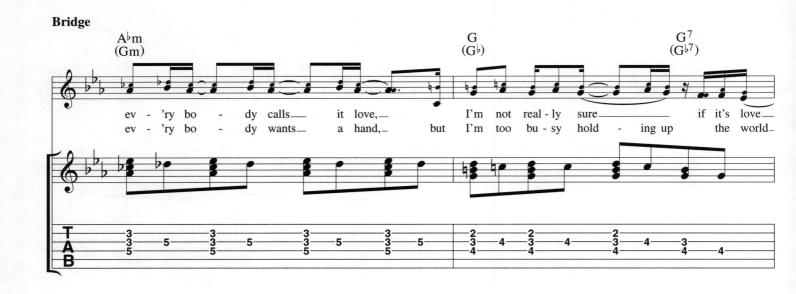

ev - 'ry bo - dy calls___ it love,___ I'm not real - ly sure_____ if it's love___
ev - 'ry bo - dy wants___ a hand,___ but I'm too bu - sy hold - ing up the world___

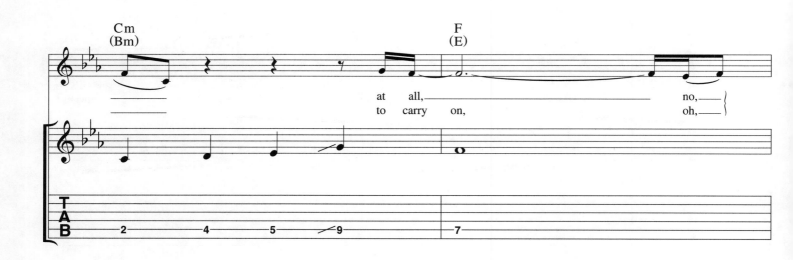

___ at all,___ no,___
___ to carry on, oh,___

To Coda ⊕

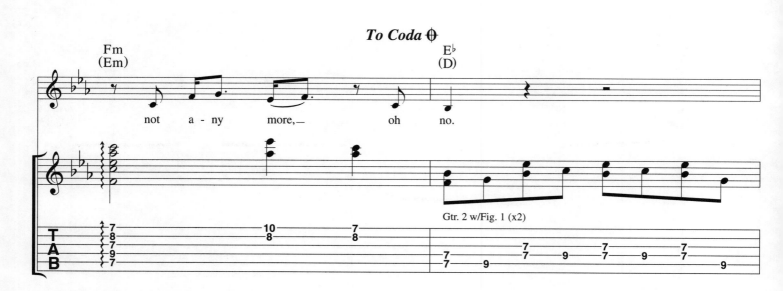

not a - ny more,___ oh no.

Gtr. 2 w/Fig. 1 (x2)

72

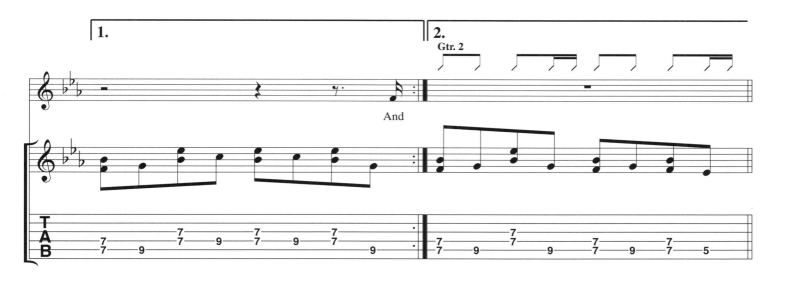

Middle

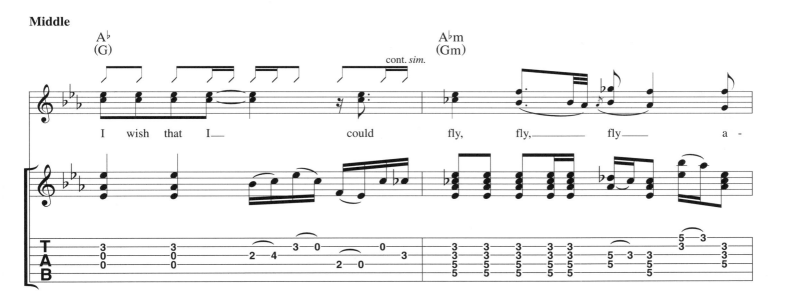

I wish that I— could fly, fly,———— fly—— a-

way. And

74

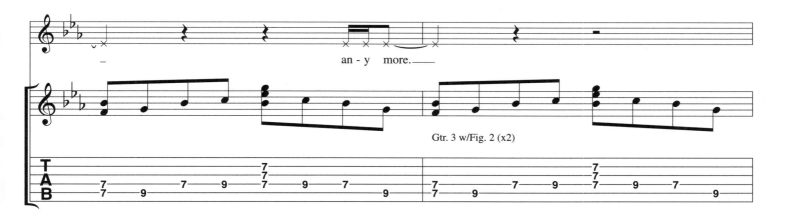

Gtr. 3 w/Fig. 2 (x2)

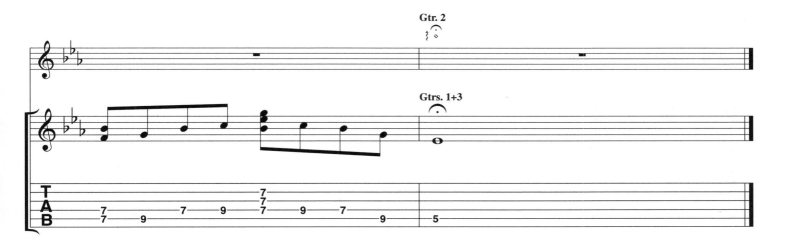

Gtr. 2

Gtrs. 1+3

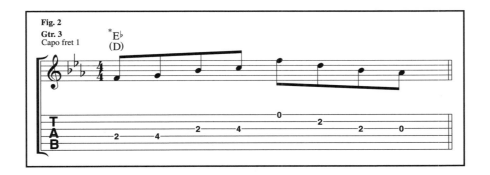

Fig. 2

Gtr. 3
Capo fret 1

*E♭
(D)

Verse 3 (𝄋):

More than us and we are them
But they don't know what's in our heads
It's more than you and it's more than I

Happy

Words & Music by Fran Healy

*Symbols in parentheses represent chord names with respect to capoed gtr. (Tab 0 = capo 3rd fret)
Symbols above represent actual sounding chords

starts in the mor - ning, when you're ly - ing next to me.
ear - ly this eve - ning, I wan - ted to be with you.

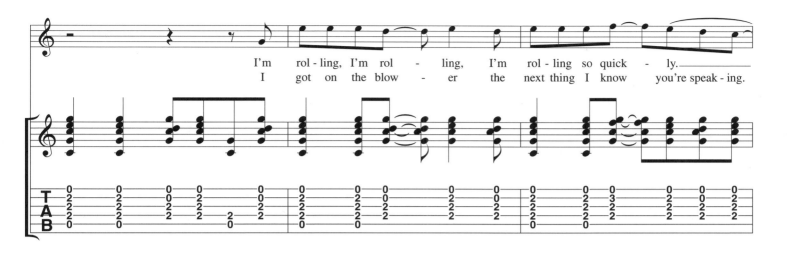

I'm rol - ling, I'm rol - ling, I'm rol - ling so quick - ly.
I got on the blow - er the next thing I know you're speak - ing.

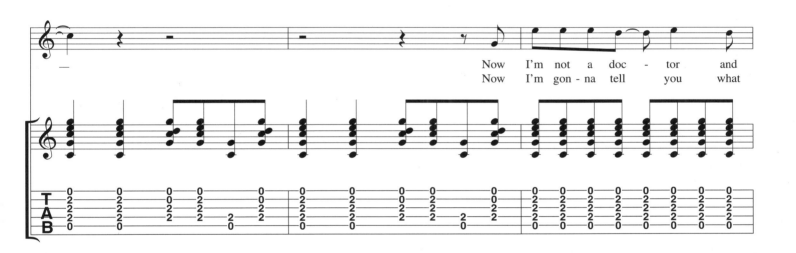

Now I'm not a doc - tor and
Now I'm gon - na tell you what

F
(D)

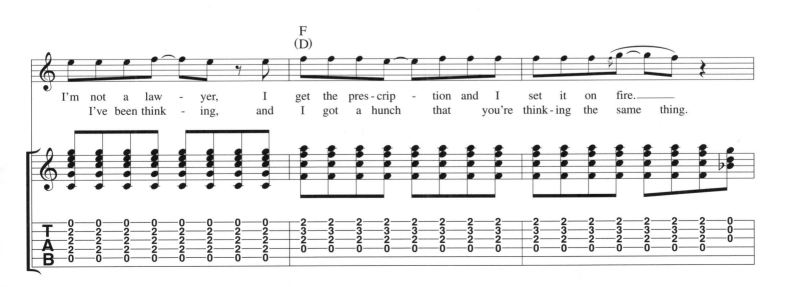

I'm not a law - yer, I get the pres - crip - tion and I set it on fire.
I've been think - ing, and I got a hunch that you're think - ing the same thing.

Blow me a kiss,___ I'll be hap - py the rest___ of my life.
And with some luck,___ we'll be ly - in' to - geth - er to - night.

And

Chorus

I'm so hap - py 'cause you're so hap - py.

I'm___ so hap - py 'cause you're so hap - py.

81

82

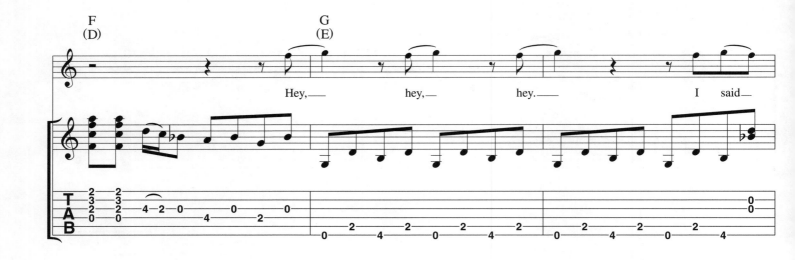

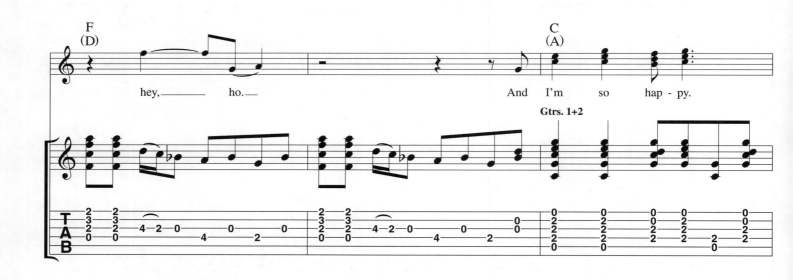

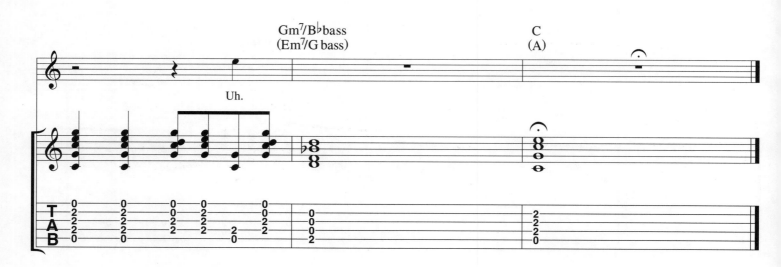

Falling Down

Words & Music by Fran Healy

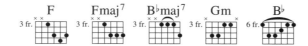

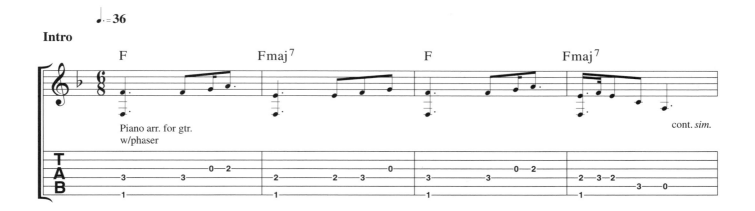

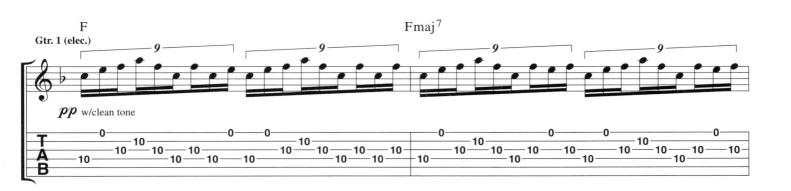

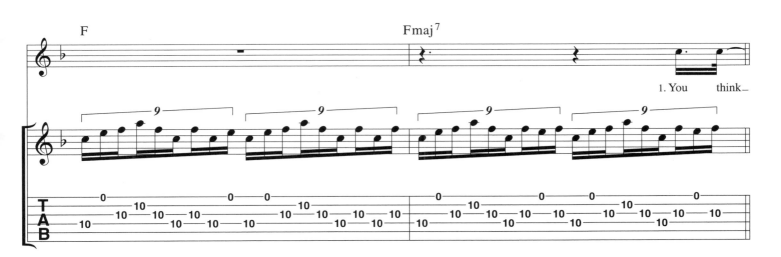

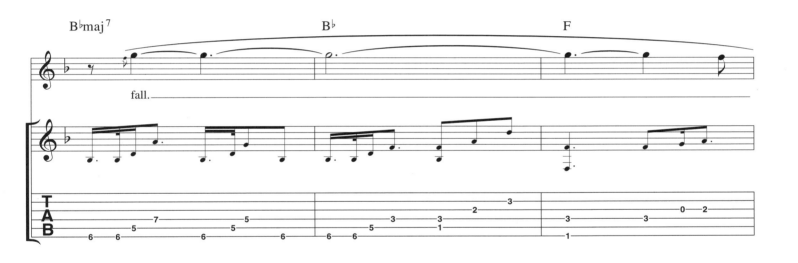

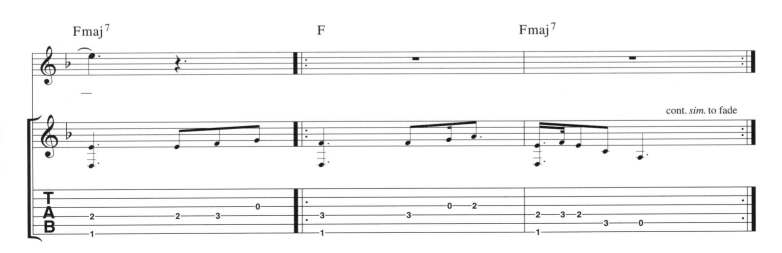

Funny Thing

Words & Music by Fran Healy

the doors. It's not fun-ny an - y - more. Ah.

Fun - ny thing to do.

w/pick up selector *
(w/feedback)

* note is struck once, but resounded by p/u switch,
turn the volume control of neck p/u to 0

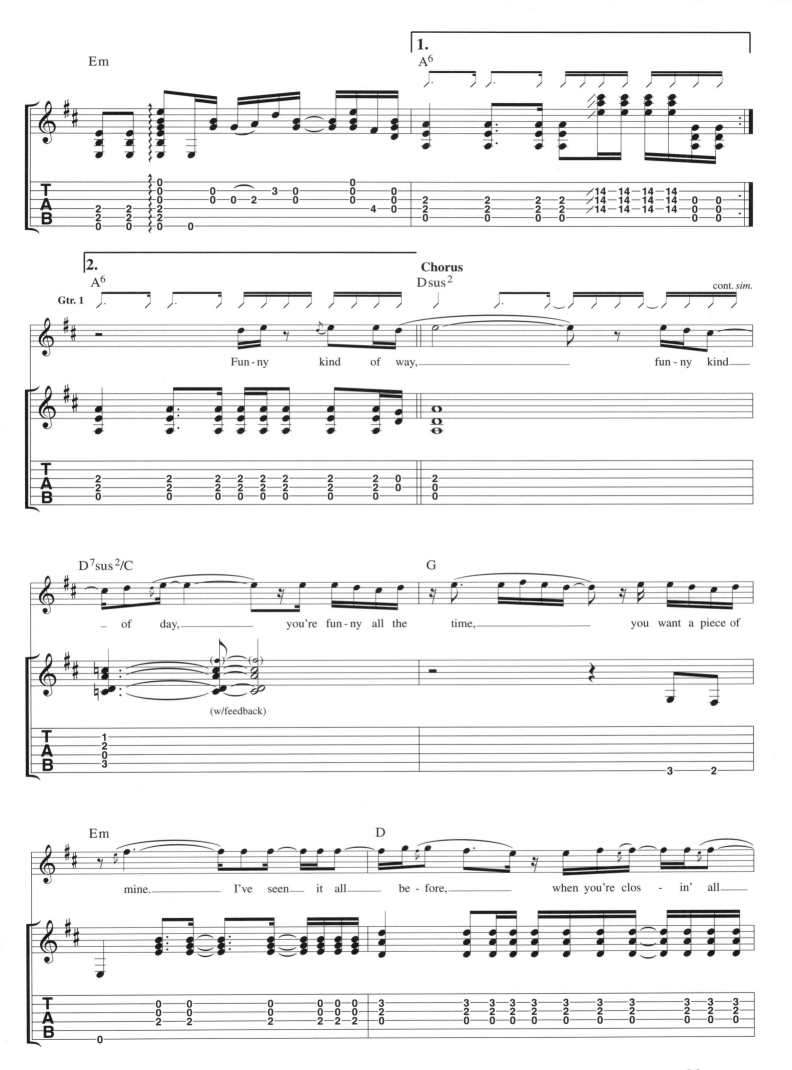

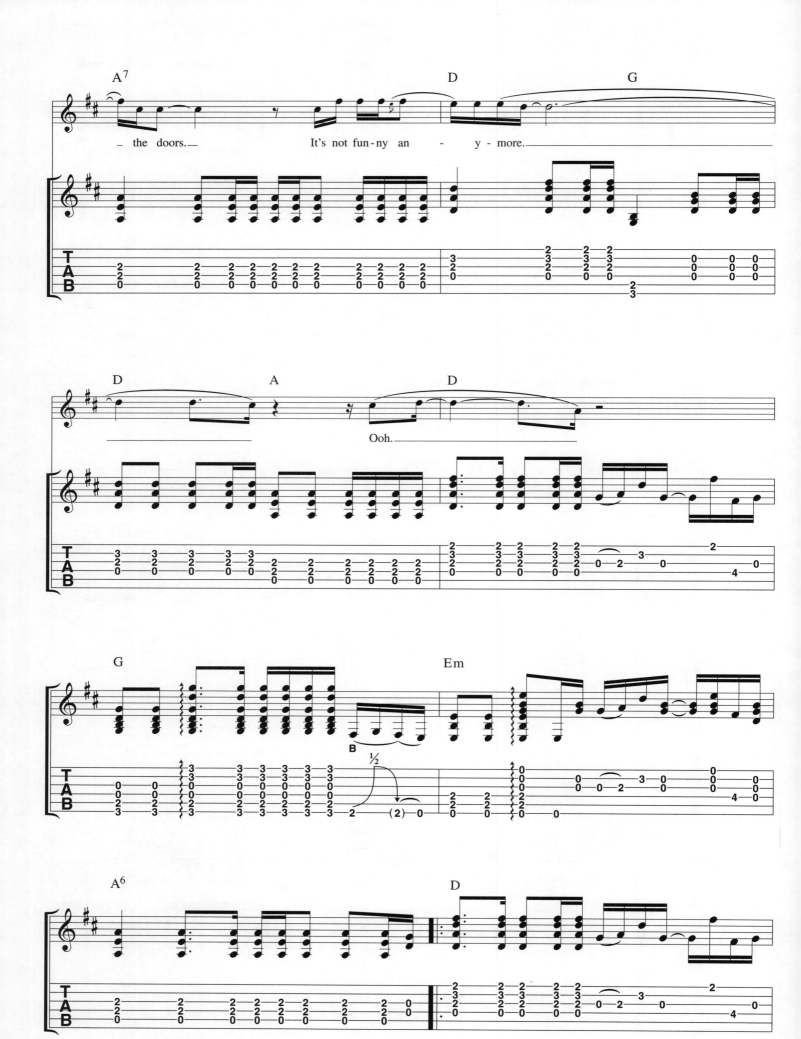

the doors.___ It's not fun-ny an - y-more.___

Ooh.___

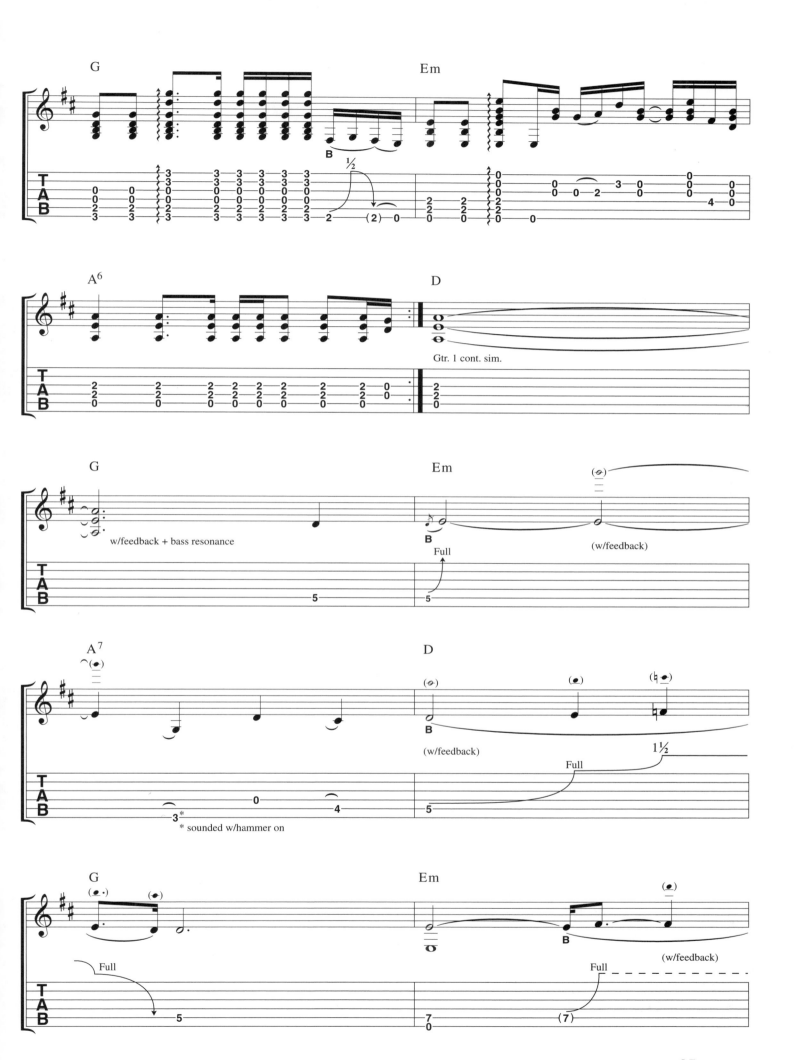

Outro

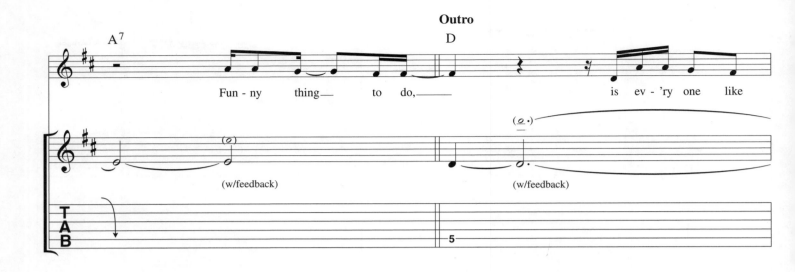

Fun - ny thing____ to do,____ is ev - 'ry one like

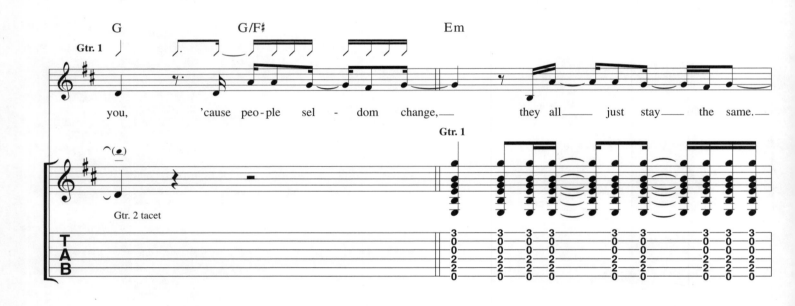

you, 'cause peo - ple sel - dom change,____ they all____ just stay____ the same.

Gtr. 2 tacet

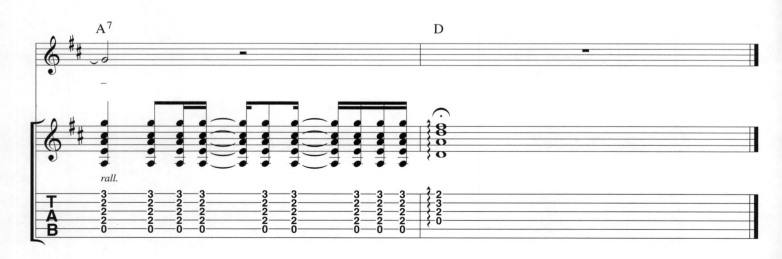

rall.

96